This book is dedicated to all who find Nature not an adversary to conquer and destroy, but a storehouse of infinite knowledge and experience linking man to all things past and present. They know conserving the natural environment is essential to our future well-being.*

ACADIA

THE STORY BEHIND THE SCENERY®

by Robert Rothe

Robert Rothe, now retired, was a National Park Service career employee. After obtaining his master's degree in environmental education administration at George Williams College in Chicago, Bob spent many years interpreting natural wonders and historic areas to visitors. As chief park naturalist at Acadia National Park he developed a keen love of this park.

Acadia National Park, *located on the coast of Maine, was first established as Lafayette NP in 1919 to preserve the natural beauty of Mount Desert Island, Isle au Haut, and Schoodic Peninsula.*

Front cover: Coastline at sunrise, photo by Glenn Van Nimwegen. Inside front cover: Bass Harbor Head Lighthouse, photo by Ron Gustafson. Page 1: Gull in flight; Pages 2/3: Early morning gilds Acadia; photos by Ed Elvidge.

Book design by K. C. DenDooven.

ACADIA: THE STORY BEHIND THE SCENERY. © 1979 KC PUBLICATIONS, INC.
"The Story Behind the Scenery"; "in pictures... The Continuing Story"; the parallelogram forms and colors within are registered in the U.S. Patent and Trademark Office.
LC 78-78121. ISBN 0-916122-57-3.

Acadia—"mountains that come down to the ocean...granite cliffs alongside which the biggest ship could ride...bays dotted with lovely islets clothed in hardwood and hemlock, altogether such a sweep of rugged coastline as has no parallel from Florida to the Canadian provinces!"— FREEMAN TILDEN

The all-pervading sea is the essence of that part of the world known as *Acadia,* dominating the land with its moods, defining and redefining the shoreline with its restless tides. In this enchanting place, whose very name sets us to dreaming of romantic sagas of the past, lies Acadia National Park, a 35,000-acre preserve of natural beauty situated on Mount Desert Island, Isle au Haut, and Schoodic Peninsula, on the coast of Maine.

From the sea come most of the sights and sounds we associate with this park: A lobster boat knifes through a murky curtain of fog; a bell buoy tolls a mournful cadence; a squadron of arriving gulls cries its haunting song. The sea, obeying its only master the wind, rises and falls on the rugged, rocky shore, and white plumes of spray mark the front line in the ageless contest between sea and land.

We stand at dawn on the summit of Cadillac Mountain, at 1,530 feet the highest point on the Atlantic coast. During the night, fog had blanketed the islands in an envelope of ethereal down, but now the morning sun lifts and banishes it into oblivion. Hostages of the night, now released, are revealed in a glorious vista of islands, coves, and bays sheltering tiny vessels bobbing in the wind. Far out at sea "a sail conceives and grows full-bellied with the wanton wind," while in the mountain air the white-throated sparrow pensively whistles its "Old Sam Peabody, Peabody, Peabody," the theme song of Acadia.

Across Frenchman Bay, the stony finger of Schoodic Peninsula (the only part of the park on the mainland) points out to sea. Beyond Blue Hill Bay, beyond Swans Island, lies Isle au Haut, the farthest outpost of Acadia.

Closer at hand is the half-lit world of the woodlands, whose timid denizens go about their business accompanied by the music of the pines —harps strummed by a whimsical wind. Carriage roads, reminding one of the gracious pursuits of days long past, wind their graceful way through the forests and around sylvan lakes, avoiding the highways and the excesses of the motor cars, to emerge high on the shoulder of another mountain. Bridges that look as if placed there by nature herself cross brooks and streams that seem to come from the idyllic dreams of childhood.

This is Acadia—a place for poets to write about and to make poets of us all.

Seen through eyes restricted by knowledge of their own mortality, the mountains, the "everlasting hills" of this beautiful land, seem to have existed always. But even as we gaze upon their gentle contours, they are changing. The landscape that is Acadia today is but one scene in a "motion picture" that has been running for millions of years. Its beginnings are indistinctly glimpsed through a curtain of ages to a time when—long before tides erased man's first foot-

A Signature of Time

print at Sand Beach, before waves clawed into Thunder Hole, even before sunbeams first caressed the gentle slopes of Cadillac Mountain —nameless rivers transported sand, silt, and mud onto the floor of an ancient sea.

These sediments built gradually (at a rate of about one inch every hundred years) until they had accreted to depths of thousands of feet. Pressure and heat transformed these sediments into the earliest bedrock that lay under what is now

the northern coast of Maine.

Next, about 500 million years ago—somewhere in the black recesses of a time too remote to comprehend—titanic forces lifted, warped, and twisted the bedrock of the sea into a mountain range whose outline towered high above today's horizon, a range perhaps as mighty as the Rockies. But, mercilessly and inexorably, the forces of air, water, gravity, and pressure ground these mountains down—grain by grain, particle by

The long arm of a diabase dike reaches out to sea at Schoodic Peninsula. It originated as molten material, flowed into an open fracture of pink granite, then cooled and solidified. Its numerous joints, or fractures, cause it to erode more rapidly than adjacent rocks. Dikes are common throughout the park and may range to more than fifty feet in width.

The face of Cadillac Mountain ages under the ceaseless onslaught of water and ice. These elements, toiling through time, dislodge bits and pieces of rock that collect in the granite's furrows, trapping soil and moisture that nourish tiny but hardy plants.

GLENN VAN NIMWEGEN

particle, rock by rock, until little was left. Today, only schists and gneisses, rocks of the Ellsworth formation, remain as testimony to those mountains of long ago.

Again, the pattern of deposition repeated itself. Rivers laden with rock fragments dislodged from adjacent lands poured their cargoes into the sea, where waves and current churned and rounded the rocks into stones and pebbles that amassed as gravel beds on the ocean floor. In the patient cycle of geologic time, streams discharged blizzards of sand and silt over the gravel, cover-

ing it to depths that probably measured in the hundreds of feet, and pressure transformed this material into solid rock. The gravel become conglomerate and the silt, siltstone. Known as the Bar Harbor formation, these deposits roofed over the earlier formation.

And yet a third time, the land that would surface as Acadia sank beneath the sea. Volcanoes belched out their contents of ash and tuff (particles less than four millimeters in size) that came to rest on the sea bottom. During the time when seaweeds still dominated the plant world, pressure and heat transformed these sediments into rocks known as the Cranberry Island formation.

Geologists sometimes refer to the Ellsworth, Bar Harbor, and Cranberry Island formations as "weak" rock. This rock, however, is not weak, except when compared to granite (the rock most common at Acadia), which is much more resistant to erosion.

A period of crustal quiet followed the deposition of the first three formations, but deep within the earth, in that domain of enormous heat and pressure, molten rock *(magma)* was preparing to intrude, dispossess, reshape, and transform the rock beds overhead. (Heat and pressure deep within the earth keep magma in a "doughy" form. Exactly where and how the heat is produced is not known; geologists speculate that radioactive minerals "decay" into other substances, over long periods of time, and produce heat in the process. Heat may also result from chemical activity in the earth's crust and from underground friction. Whatever that heat source may be, it results in a magma temperature ranging from one to two thousand degrees F.)

Magma invaded the weak-rock formations above it at least four times, over prolonged periods of time. The first of these intrusions produced *diorite*. Although most of the magma congealed beneath the surface, some poured out above ground as *lava*. Then followed three enormous bodies of magma that solidified into granite—first a fine-grained, then a coarse-grained, and finally a medium-grained granite. The fine-grained granite resulted from magma that cooled in a relatively short time; the others from magma that cooled more slowly.

Each of the intrusions altered the overhead bedrock both chemically and physically, but the most dramatic change was that in which the coarse-grained granite was formed. This activity was not an isolated phenomenon; it was in fact part of an extensive intrusion *(batholith)* that reached from what is now New Brunswick on the east to Penobscot Bay on the west, a distance of about a hundred miles. This invasion completely "remodeled" the geological architecture of the Mount Desert Island region.

Far below the earth's surface, the magma cooked and churned. A huge, molasseslike plug of magma at least eight miles in diameter moved upward. And as it undermined the overlying bedrock, the heavy roof rocks began to sag and rupture, eventually sinking and melting into the magma. The fiery mass incorporated material from an earlier granitic formation (fine-grained

GLENN VAN NIMWEGEN

Above the intense blue waters of the Atlantic stand the forested slopes of Gorham Mountain, Champlain Mountain, and the Beehive. Acadia's uplands are the highest along the entire Eastern Seaboard.

ED COOPER

granite), from diorite, and from the weak rocks. This enormous block of various types of matter did not fall sharply from the adjacent walls and ceiling; instead it shattered into a chaotic mass of rock fragments, called *breccia*. Evicting and then consuming the overlying rock, magma filled the cavity and gradually cooled to form the coarse-grained granite.

After the various granites developed, other minor intrusions of magmatic material occurred. The most conspicuous of these consisted of diabase *dikes* that wedged themselves into open fractures in older rock. Schoodic Peninsula's granite embraces the most obvious examples of these formations in the park.

The motion picture of geologic history rushes on—past the appearance of the first insects, the first reptiles, even beyond the time when dinosaurs dominated all of life, including that alien group the mammals. During this interminable period of time, erosion was the chief geological agent.

Finally a frame comes into dim focus: The Mount Desert region appears as a plain, with only an occasional low mountain to relieve the land's flat profile. A closer look reveals that the agents of erosion—rivers, rain, weathering—have removed the overlying rocks from Mount Desert, and the various granites, more resistant to erosion, have emerged to form its central core. Sur-

rounding this massive center, a fringe of weak rock encircles the base of the granite highlands. Seen too is the *shatter zone,* a narrow rim marking the violent welding of the coarse granite with adjacent rock formations.

These mountains don't look like the familiar ones of the Mount Desert Range. Instead of consisting of solitary mountains separated by deep valleys, the range is one continuous ridge. Instead of forming steep slopes, the mountains' flanks are gentle in profile and serve as wellheads for slow-running streams.

But soon the land begins to rise and tilt slightly toward the sea. As the land's posture changes, gravity reactivates stream-flow throughout the region. Measured in the unhurried cadence of geologic time, the rivers cut *V*-shaped valleys into the face of the range. But there the geologic picture begins to fade; it will not appear sharp and clear again until the coming of the ice ages, a period not far removed from our own, at least in the reckoning of geologic time.

An Odyssey of Ice

In 1837 the young Swiss naturalist Louis Agassiz astonished the scientific community by announcing that huge glaciers once covered large sections of northern Europe. Astonishment quickly subsided to amusement as the scientists of the day stoutly and derisively rejected this threat to dearly held beliefs. But Agassiz would eventually triumph, for the evidence to support his theory was unshakable, evidence that was scattered all over northern Europe in the form of heaped moraines of sand and gravel, of rock beds grooved and scratched, of displaced boulders, of U-shaped valleys and many other "signatures" left by the moving glaciers.

Agassiz came to America in 1846, took a professorship at Harvard, and taught zoology and geology there for twenty-seven years. After a visit to Maine and Mount Desert Island in 1864, he wrote, in his *Geological Sketches*: "Mount Desert . . . must have been a miniature Spitzbergen, and colossal icebergs floated off from Somes Sound into the Atlantic Ocean, as they do nowadays from Magdelena Bay. . . ." and: "We are . . . justified in supposing that the icefields, when they poured from the north over New England to the sea, had a thickness of at least five or six thousand feet."

Ice that thick? It seems impossible, but the idea is intriguing. What known object could be compared to that colossus of ice? Cadillac Mountain stands at 1,530 feet. If we can imagine three or four such mountains, one atop the other, then we may be able to visualize the thickness of the ice estimated by Agassiz. Even with sophisticated techniques available to geologists today, we are still uncertain of the ice thickness; estimates range between three thousand and nine thousand feet.

What caused such an enormity of ice to form? Various geologic and astronomic theories have been offered in attempts to explain the cause, but none are accepted universally. One traditional theory holds that a nucleus of ice began to expand about seventy thousand years ago and, over a period of thirty thousand years, grew to envelop about thirty percent of the earth's surface. But recent analysis of ocean-floor sediments challenges this theory; the data obtained suggests that the ice mass reached its maximum size in only *nine* thousand years.

A second theory accounts for the rapid and widespread appearance of the glaciers by contending that not only the Far North but also vast regions of the Northern Hemisphere were plunged into a climatic freeze. Snowfields expanded and combined as the weather turned cold; new snow piled upon old and the sun's heat failed to melt it as fast as it accumulated; thus almost a third of the planet became rapidly (geologically speaking) enshrouded in ice.

During the last two to three million years, ice sheets intermittently covered most of New

GLENN VAN NIMWEGEN

Autumn's colors soften the abrupt east face of Champlain Mountain, sheared by glaciers. The rock wall, known as the "Precipice," towers more than a thousand feet high.

England. Because each succeeding glacier scraped away signs of earlier glaciations, it is the last glacier that has left the most pronounced impact on Acadia's landscape today. As the last glacier expanded out of Canada and spread across New England, the weight of thousands of winters of ice (a single acre of ice one mile thick weighs almost seven million tons) caused the land beneath to depress. The enormous weight compressed the ice, and individual crystals slipped and rolled, pushing and sliding over one another.

The ice mass moved, and on its way it leveled hilltops, excavated soil, flattened forests, and dug new drainage systems. When the leading edge of the glacier reached the highlands of Mount Desert, it probably banked its ice against the northern flank of the mountains before con-

Transported by an ice sheet from a ledge at least twenty miles to the northwest, this huge boulder (erratic) now perches on Cadillac Mountain above Frenchman Bay and the Porcupine Islands.

tinuing its forward progress. But then, like dough rising over the lip of a pan, it surged into one and then another notch in the mountain crests, until six or eight tongues of ice probed the stream-cut valleys. They moved like very slow rivers, but even at the speed of only a few inches or a few feet a day, the strength of the ice far surpassed that of any river.

As the tireless sculptor cut deeper and wider, not even granite could resist it. The glacier's speed increased as it flowed through the narrow waists of the valleys. Just as a river intensifies its erosional power in the narrows, so did the ice multiply its capacity to excavate. Eventually— after the ice wasted away—some of these deepened valleys became water basins, filling hollows that would become such beautiful waters as Eagle Lake and Echo Lake. In one instance it cut a trough that must have resulted from an ice-sculpting "binge." (Now filled with sea water, Somes Sound is considered by many geologists to be a *fiord*, albeit a poorly developed one.)

The placid waters of Jordan Pond fill a basin scoured by glacial ice. Above it swell the gentle contours of North Bubble and South Bubble.

After the ice forged through the valleys, its main body rose high over the mountain range and buried it under the pressure of incalculable tons of ice. Impelled up the northern slopes, the grinding mass streamlined and rounded the profile of the mountain range from base to summit, while on the southern slopes it chiseled out giant steps. Flowing stiffly down the abrupt inclines toward the sea, the bottom ice adopted the shape of the slope. But the upper ice did not keep pace, and its back was broken into a series of cracks, or crevasses. Melting water ran into the crevasses, seeped into fractures, and froze the rock face against the ice mass. As the glacier continued its downward creep, it plucked fractured rock from the cliff sides, leaving them jagged and precipitous—a dramatic landscape for visitors of the future to view and marvel at.

The great ice sheet did not travel alone. Embedded within its mass was a passenger load of sand, stone, and grit—tools with which the glacier etched scratches in the granite or polished its rough face smooth. On its broad back the glacier conveyed boulders as big as trucks, plucking them from mountain ridges, hauling them along, and then dumping them one by one at places far distant from their origins, thus gaining for them the term *erratics*. The most conspicuous of these in the park is the mammoth rock that rests near the summit of South Bubble Mountain. This erratic is easily identified from the park road.

The glacier not only carved valleys and rounded mountains, but also withheld enormous quantities of water from the oceans by entrapping it in the form of ice. For untold centuries water evaporated, formed clouds, and precipitated as snow—snow that did not return to the ocean but rather metamorphosed into ice, adding to the glacier's size and weight. Beneath this enormous burden, the earth compressed about one foot for each three feet of ice pressing down upon it.

Then, about eighteen thousand years ago, the ice mass stopped growing. It had reached the contintental shelf a hundred and fifty miles or so south of Mount Desert Island when climatic patterns altered and a warming trend halted its progress. Heat became a formidable enemy of the glacier; the great destroyer was itself being destroyed. Cliffs of ice broke from its snout and rivers gushed from its massive bulk. The leading edge of the glacier was now its tail, in retreat

GLENN VAN NIMWEGEN

MARIE MENZIETTI

Acadia's coastline is a scene of never-ending strife between land and water. Waves assail the coast with their booming might. The impassive rocks resist but pay to their restless adversary a continuing ransom in sand and stone.

Sustained by an autumn downpour and impelled by gravity, a temporary freshet on Cadillac Mountain cascades in a curtain of freshness, shifting small stones and stirring bright leaves in its path. Its song of joyous abandon falls on shelves of solid, unresponsive rock.

reaching central Maine about four thousand years after having conquered the continental shelf.

Meanwhile, the sea advanced against the ice margin, flooding today's coastline to a depth of about three hundred feet. The earth's crust, freed of its burden of ice, started to rebound; the sea, now unable to hold its position on the land, withdrew. The resilient land continued to rise relative to the sea until about ten thousand years ago, when it finally stabilized. Since that time, the level of the sea worldwide has risen to its present height, and it continues to rise at a rate of about two inches per century. The rising sea and downwarped land mass create a situation referred to as "drowned coast." This simply means that what appears today as arms and fingers of the sea were once river valleys; islands were the tops of mountains; headlands and peninsulas were rocky ridges.

It is said that the Indians of Mount Desert thought the island resembled a giant lobster claw, Somes Sound representing the space between the pincers. Although this description may be very appealing to the imagination, the Indians probably never suspected that their "lobster claw" was actually a creation forged in a crucible of ice. Like the Indians, we can see only the effects of the unseen force. But partly because of the study that resulted in Louis Agassiz' bold pronouncement, we can more easily understand how bedrock became the mold from which ice carved the land now known as Acadia, gouging out valleys, warping its coastline, and softening the profiles of its mountains.

SHORE PATTERNS

The bedrock gave substance and the glaciers gave character, but without the sea Acadia would be like a gem without a setting. Each headland, bay, cove, and inlet reveals in a major or minor way the majestic interface between sea and land. Even visitors from the western states, who may chuckle at the height of the mountains here, are enthralled by the vistas of incomparable scenery Acadia offers.

Earth and water complement one another, yet they are eternal antagonists. The sea attacks and the land resists, and Acadia must bear the brunt of the enormous energies unleashed in the waves that batter her cliffs and erupt into lofty geysers. Even the headlands, the highest along the Eastern Seaboard, offer no refuge from the sea in its fiercest displays of rampaging virtuosity.

Thunder Hole is a familiar example of the awesome power of the sea. When the wind is strong, the rising tide surges into the narrow chasm, compressing the captured air and resounding with a boom that is felt as well as heard. The surging tides rotate stones—some as large as bowling balls—on the chasm floor, hurling them against the bottleneck of rock in a ceaseless effort to tunnel deeper into it. (Thunder Hole is not as predictable, however, as Yellowstone's

Old Faithful. Often when the air is motionless and the tide is low, it remains disappointingly still.)

But the tremendous energy of the sea is perhaps best demonstrated at Baker Island. Here the gently sloping granite is scored with long horizontal cracks, in which rushing water exerts leverage. Powerful waves have cut out flat slabs of rock—some as much as twenty feet long and three feet thick—as neatly as those hewn from a stone quarry. Like some mythical giant child playing with blocks, the sea has wrenched them free and piled them haphazardly into a dam forty feet above sea level. Yankee humor refers to this flat surface as "the dance floor."

The sea destroys and displaces, but it also builds. What it takes from one point on the coast it may add to another. With the irresistible energy of hammer blows, the waves dislodge rock particles, transport them, smooth them, and deposit them at the heads of nearly every cove. In still other places the dispossessed stones and cobbles become gravel bars and shoals. Bar Harbor was named for just such a bar, which connects it to Bar Island.

Because the coast is young, sandy shores are rare. But at Newport Cove (Sand Beach), shore currents have shifted the tons of sand that the sea

Clam diggers take advantage of low tide, heedless of the stately mansions along shore, romantic relics of a bygone era. The town of Bar Harbor derived its name from the gravel bar (foreground) that ties Mount Desert Island to Bar Island. Built and maintained by wave action, the bar is submerged at high tide.

eroded from the rocks. Mixed into the sand are broken bits of shells and the skeletons of crabs, mussels, sea urchins, and other marine life. In winter, storm waves often partially denude the cove, robbing it of its sediment and depositing it offshore. But the gentle waves of summer unfailingly return the sediments to Sand Beach in time to welcome the first sunbathers of the season.

The story that began with sediments piled on the floor of a primordial sea closes for the moment with those washed ashore at Sand Beach. Each represents a phase in a geologic cycle as old as the earth itself, a cycle of rocks forming and disintegrating. But in reality there is no beginning and no ending, only creation and destruction, renewal and ruin. Rock becomes sand; sand becomes rock. The granite of Cadillac Mountain, the cobbles at Hunters Cove, even a pinch of grit at Sand Beach bears witness to this timeless cycle. For indelibly written on the landscape, in bold strokes or fine scratches, is a script that tells the astonishing story of mountain ranges that rose and fell, of coastlines that emerged and vanished, of ice that sealed in a continent.

SUGGESTED READING

CHAPMAN, CARLETON A. *The Geology of Acadia National Park.* New York: The Chatham Press, Inc., 1970.

ED ELVIDGE

Those Who Came Before . . .

Many hundreds of years before European adventurers discovered the beautiful harboring bays and inlets of this Maine island, a Stone Age people, the Abnaki Indians, knew Mount Desert as their home. They called it *Pemetic*, "the sloping land." Members of the Penobscot and Passamaquoddy tribes of the Algonquian language family, the Abnaki survived in the wilderness.

Their simple culture owed much to the white birch tree, from which the women stripped the bark to fashion wigwams, baskets, and other implements of daily living. From this tree also came the birch-bark canoe, "light and beautiful and yet so strong that they trusted their lives to it when they shot the rock-fanged rapids." This graceful conveyance was so much a part of their lives, it is not surprising that the early French explorers called these Indians *Etchemins*, "people of the canoe."

Depending in part on the accuracy of their arrows and the tautness of their snares, moose, deer, and seabirds provided meat, hides, feathers, and bone utensils. Riches of the sea offered fish, lobster, and clams. Having intimate knowledge of forest greenery, Abnaki Indians collected plants and berries. Yet life was harsh and villages remained small; archaeologists estimate that the coastal Maine Indian population numbered between ten thousand and fifteen thousand in the early 1600s.

Between 1616 and 1620, an epidemic of European origin swept northeasterly along the Maine coast. In many Indian communities, the mortality rate reached 50 to 100 percent, devastating the social fabric of Indian society. Therefore personal accounts written by seventeenth-, eighteenth- and nineteenth-century explorers and settlers describe the Indian lifestyle that emerged only after the epidemic—a lifestyle that developed in response to European influence. To understand Indian life before the influx of Europeans, scientists examine archaeological evidence, often concentrated in coastal shell middens, prehistoric garbage dumps laden with broken clam and mussel shells, arrowheads, pottery fragments, and bones.

The Abnaki, standing on the threshold of historic times, had been preceded here by other Native Americans. Although records are scanty, deep shell heaps testify to Indian encampments dating back seven thousand years. The fate of these people can only be guessed at; perhaps the Abnaki destroyed them, or perhaps they quite naturally evolved or were assimilated into that group of Indians.

The first meeting between the people of Pemetic and those of the European continent is also a matter of conjecture, since historical records shed no light on this event. Some say that Norsemen—perhaps Leif Ericson himself—were the first white men here; others postulate that fishermen from Portugal or Normandy who were fishing off the Grand Banks and blown off course were the first Europeans to alight here.

A legacy from the American Indian, a canoe lightly skims the surface of Bubble Pond.

RUSSELL D. BUTCHER

A filmy veil of mist enshrouds Bass Harbor Head Lighthouse.

Of more consequence, at any rate, was the trip made by Giovanni da Verrazzano, an Italian navigator who sailed on behalf of Francis I of France. After a seven-week voyage from the coast of Africa, he reached landfall near Cape Fear, North Carolina, in March, 1524. It is doubtful that he came within miles of Pemetic, but his influence was felt here even so, since it was he who seems to have originated the term *Arcadia*. The sylvan beauty of the new land he saw must have reminded him of descriptions of the idealized Arcadian landscape of ancient Greece. By 1600, cartographers, ignorant of North American geography, had remade maps, moving Arcadia steadily north-eastward to include the lands of Maine, New Brunswick, and Nova Scotia. These same map makers shortened the name to *Acadie*, or sometimes *Lacadia*, *L'Acadie*, or *La Cadie*.

NEW FRANCE

But it was a Frenchman, Samuel Champlain, who made the first important contribution to the historical record of Mount Desert Island. It was he who led the expedition that landed in Pemetic on September 5, 1604. History does not record whether the Abnaki actually watched the strange vessel approach. But if they did, they were probably guardedly watchful—and perhaps even amused when it struck a shoal off Otter Point. The beached voyagers came ashore, repaired their boat, and after an interval in which some reluctance on the part of the Indians had to be overcome, the men from France met the men from Pemetic.

The primary duty of the Frenchmen was to find a location in the New World for a permanent settlement, but they also wanted to affirm the generations-old tale of *Norumbega*, the legendary walled city of precious metal and crystal. What if anything the Indians may have said about Norumbega is not known, but they were an amiable people, anxious to please and fond of telling tall tales, and doubtless they saw no harm in perpetuating the myth of the grand city. (If Indians were not in fact the originators of this tale, perhaps it was a glorious yarn spun from the imagination of David Ingram, who had trudged up the Maine coast and, once back in England, had paid his tavern bills by satisfying his contemporaries' thirst for the fantastic.)

But Champlain, to his credit, was not taken in by tales of wealthy kingdoms or promises of gold and jewels; he later wrote: "I am convinced that the majority of those that mention [Norumbega] never saw it and speak of it only by

"To everything there is a season, and a time for every purpose." At Acadia, each season brings nature's art into focus in an abundance of bright hues; but it is the spring and autumn, most observers would agree, in which Acadia's plant life is at its most resplendent.

MARIE MENZIETTI

Rhodora, lover of wet lands

Cardinal flower, a favorite framed by birches

ED FLYINGE

MARIE MENZIETTI

Shadbush, or serviceberry: harbinger of spring

Water lily, fragrant American native

TED GRINDLE

SACILOTTO-HINKE

Mountain ash, on Cadillac Mountain

Wild lupine, another hallmark of spring

Northern-red-oak leaves, a brilliant montage

RUSSELL D. BUTCHER

MARIE MENZIETTI

hearsay...." Champlain was a practical man who wrote only of things he observed and experienced. Accordingly, his journal speaks of the island called called Pemetic, which he renamed l'Isle des Monts-deserts," and Mount Desert Island it still is. This name literally translates as the "Isle of Bare Mountains," but Champlain's usage of the word *desert* in his other writings leads one to suspect that he meant it simply to describe a desolate, unexplored region devoid of habitation rather than vegetation.

Champlain had made that voyage at an early stage in his life, before he went on to found Quebec and earn his place in history. He had crossed the Atlantic when a young man, as pilot and geographer to Pierre Duque, Sieur de Mons, a Huguenot gentleman who had found favor with Henry IV, King of France. Impelled by motivations stemming from national rivalries, material gain, and his own spirit of adventure, the king had commissioned de Mons as Lieutenant Gen-

eral of New France, granting him a ten-year fur-trading monopoly there and a mandate to colonize the new world. His patent authorized de Mons "to represent our person in the lands and territories...of Acadia, to commence at the fortieth degree of latitude and extend to the forty-sixth degree."

It was thus armed with a grandiose commission and the considerable talents of his protege Champlain that de Mons and his retinue sailed from France and in due course chose Dochet Island (now St. Croix Island National Monument) as a temporary settlement. It was from there that Champlain set out with a crew of 12 to explore the rocky coast and study the inhabitants.

Champlain continued his explorations as far as Pemaquid Bay before returning to St. Croix on October 2 and the onset of the cruel winter of 1604-05, which struck the settlement a blow from which it never recovered. Before spring came, nearly half of the 79 Frenchmen lay buried in the island's cemetery, a tragedy that convinced de

A winter storm transforms trees and ledges into a dazzling snowscape along Ocean Drive. At the shoreline, bare rock measures the level of high tide.

Bespattered by chilling storm waves, a low-lying shrub is wrapped in a crackling crown of icicles. However beautiful her works of art, nature is ever practical; the ice insulates the plants from bitter winter winds.

Mons to abandon St. Croix and search for another location. By August 1605, he had established a new colony at Port Royal, now Annapolis Royal, Nova Scotia.

The visit of the Frenchmen to Acadia 16 years before the Pilgrims landed at Plymouth Rock destined the country to become known as "New France" before it became "New England." Champlain's maps of landfalls and his charts of harbors gave future mariners a reliable guide, for this resourceful navigator could draw a map so precise that, unlike most maps of the day, sailors could actually locate a specific place on a second trip. (Champlain himself made 29 crossings of the Atlantic—14 round trips and a final one-way journey—before his death in Quebec on Christmas Day, 1635.) Acadia's Champlain Mountain immortalizes the dauntless adventurer, and it is a fitting tribute to a son of old France who became the "Father of New France."

Meanwhile, King Henry IV had been assassinated and Louis XIII had ascended the French throne. With this event de Mons lost his position of strength in the New World. His patent was bought by Antionette de Pons, the Marquise de Guercheville, and was enlarged to include all of North America to the Gulf of Mexico. Her dream was to establish a Jesuit mission colony in the New World. The marquise was a person of considerable wealth and sterling virtue. (In her youth she had with impunity resisted the amorous advances of Henry IV.) In late life now and fired by religious zeal, she declared herself protectress of the American missions. It was as her instrument that the ill-fated ship, ominously named the *Jonas,* set sail from Hosfleur, France, bound for Kadisquit (Bangor).

As the *Jonas,* after touching briefly at Port Royal, neared the coast of Maine, it became enveloped in a terrifying fog. The fifty or so passengers, uncertain of deliverance, took refuge in prayer, led by their spiritual mentor, the Jesuit priest Father Pierre Biard. Two days and nights had passed when finally the dawn broke clear and the devout company found itself at anchor off Mount Desert, in the calm waters of Frenchman Bay, near what is now Bar Harbor.

Hardly was there time to give thanks to God, row ashore, and name the place *St. Sauveur* before smoke signals announced the presence of Indians. The Abnaki, who had always been on good terms with the French, came to greet them, persistently urging them to set sail around to Somes Sound and settle there instead. It was "quite as good a place as Kadisquit," they said. Besides, their chief, Asticou, lay mortally ill at

Fog moves in and twirls its murky wreath around a lobster boat. As one lobsterman observed, "The fog is so thick ye cud stick your knife in it to mark the passage back."

that place and desired baptism. Faced with such a touching exhortation, how could Father Biard refuse? He gave in and had the Indians paddle him around to the chief's village near the entrance to the sound, only to discover that Asticou suffered from nothing more severe than a head cold.

But the clever ploy of Asticou had worked. Once there, the Jesuits needed little convincing to establish their mission here instead; the pleasant, grassy aspect of the place was invitation enough. So it was that across from the Indian village and separated from it by Somes Sound, the Jesuits, after the *Jonas* was brought around, raised their cross and pitched their tents, and St. Sauveur was transferred to the site known today as Fernald Point.

ENGLAND ENFORCES ITS CLAIM

But fate was against the Frenchmen. They had just begun to build a fort, plant their corn, and baptize the natives, when the *Treasurer*, an English ship commanded by the redoubtable Captain Samuel Argall (the same one who had captured Pocahontas), bore down on them. The captain was under orders from the Governor of Virginia to search out and expel any foreigners from the territory claimed by the Virginia Company, which had been given the entire Atlantic Coast by King James I of England in 1606.

Guided to St. Sauveur by unsuspecting Indians (they thought all white men were the same), Argall's cannoneers attacked the surprised and completely unprepared settlers, and in the resulting brief skirmish three Frenchmen died, ironically including Brother Gilbert du Thet, who had once piously voiced his desire to die in the service of God. They rest at a place unknown in the soil of Mount Desert.

As the terrified Jesuits fled into the forest, Captain Argall seized the opportunity to come ashore and filch the French commission papers from the strong box. When the colonists, faced with starvation in the wilds, returned and surrendered, the wily Argall, assuming the role of an offended subject of the king, reproached them for "unauthorized entry" and demanded an entitlement, which of course the Frenchmen could not produce.

Eventually, after detainment under the threat of hanging, the "trespassers" were released by the English; even the *Jonas*, which had lived up to its unlucky name, was finally returned to Madame de Guercheville. Father Biard resumed his chair in theology at Lyons, where he was no doubt sought after by eager students who sat

Before the automobile put them out of business some 45 years ago, steamships transported vacationers to the booming resort of Bar Harbor. Canadian National's M. V. Bluenose carries on the tradition, accommodating travelers and their vehicles on its six-hour voyage between Bar Harbor and Yarmouth, Nova Scotia.

wide-eyed at the telling of his remarkable adventures in New France.

Although the English victory at Fernald Point in 1613 doomed Jesuit ambitions at Mount Desert, the English did not consolidate their prize by establishing a settlement there. In the ensuing years, the English monarch awarded grants to his "worthy constituents," but none were so imprudent as to actually take up residence in a land that lay so close to French territory.

So for the next century and a half, the island's importance was primarily its use as a landmark for seamen and pilgrims. True, there was much rivalry and some small-scale warfare between the English and the French, whose king had never given up claim to the territory. But most references to the area during this time were those contained in mariners' journals or they were poetic references such as that made by Governor Winthrop, who, leading his fleet of Puritan ships bound for Massachusetts Bay in 1630, likened the "sweet air" emanating from the Maine shore to "the smell of a garden."

The territory was thus in a state of limbo, lying as it did between the French, firmly entrenched in New France, and the British, whose settlements in Massachusetts and southward were becoming increasingly numerous.

There was a brief period when it seemed Mount Desert would again become the center of dramatic activity. In 1688 Antoine Laumet, an ambitious young man who had immigrated to New France as a young man and had bestowed upon himself the title *Sieur Antonine de la Mothe Cadillac*, sought a land grant there. His scheme was to establish a feudal estate on which he and his bride could live as "Lord and Lady of the Manor." Louis XIV's court was a spawning bed

Overleaf: Otter Cove shelters a lobster boat below mountains slumbering under a blanket of autumn mist. Photo by Glenn Van Nimwegen.

The Beehive rises above windswept marsh grass —
precinct of muskrats, red-winged blackbirds,
and other lovers of wet lands.

for such grandiose land schemes in America, and few surpassed the one proposed by Cadillac, who asked for and received 100,000 acres of land, including part of the Maine coast and all of Mount Desert.

But Cadillac's empire was to be short-lived. Although he did reside here for a time (historians disagree on the exact location), he soon abandoned his fanciful enterprise—for reasons history has never revealed. Perhaps he was too full of his other visionary plans to allow him to tarry too long in one place; perhaps his underlings balked at being serfs in a land already swept by the early winds of liberty; perhaps he and his bride found the winters too formidable.

Whatever his reasons for leaving, the elegant and witty Cadillac went on to fame as founder of the settlement that later became Detroit (where later still an automobile manufacturer picked up his name and coat of arms to promote his new motor car, now an instantly recognized symbol of prestige in any part of the country). But no matter where fortune and his wandering nature led him, he continued to sign his important documents *Seigneur de Douaquet et des Monts Déserts*, ''Lord of Frenchman Bay and Mount Desert,'' perhaps in this revealing a wistful longing that persisted for the Maine coast and the mountains, one of which now bears his name.

And, despite his failure to plant a feudal economy in the wilds of Maine, Cadillac did continue to influence events at Mount Desert. Like Champlain, he had great ability as a writer, and his reports to France concerning the island's secluded waters did not escape the attention of the navy. For almost a decade afterward, Mount Desert Island and its island-studded eastern bay (Frenchman Bay) served as a lair from which French warships pounced on English shipping and coastal towns.

The Tragedy of the Grand Design

In October 1739, Mount Desert became the scene of a terrible tragedy, when the *Grand Design*, a ship engaged in the innocent pursuit of transporting 200 Irish immigrants to Pennsylvania, was assaulted by foul weather and struck submerged rocks off the granite headlands of Ship Harbor. The luckless pilgrims escaped ashore, only to find themselves facing the approaching winter on a solitary and inhospitable coast, without adequate shelter or food. A hundred of the men set off to seek aid at some hoped-for settlement inland—none was ever heard of again.

It was not until the following March that Indians discovered the remainder of the marooned company, now suffering piteously from the extreme privations they had endured. When rescuers from the town of Warren finally got through, only a few emaciated survivors remained, among them two young women who had buried their husbands earlier that terrible winter. Both eventually married men from Warren, and their many descendants continue to live in Maine.

A Question of Ownership

The tragedy of the *Grand Design* shifted attention only momentarily from the contest between the French and English aristocracies to win control of North America. But in 1759, after nearly a century and a half of war and of armed truces masquerading as peace, British arms finally triumphed at Quebec, ending French dominion in Acadia and Canada.

Land titles of prominent French Quebec families were little affected by the English victory, but the Indians, who had always been looked upon as friends of the French and as such were targets for the English, were obliged to move deeper into the woods of the interior, leaving their homes and lands forever. With the frontier safe, the Indians scattered, and the fleur-de-lis

An autumn storm vents its fury on the rock-rimmed coast. That ''queen of flowers'' the wild rose grows defiantly in a stark stone garden.

banished, the lands along the Maine coast were now up for grabs, and Boston land speculators looked with interest upon this territory, which bore only faintly the marks of the explorers, missionaries, and adventurers who had touched here.

Governor Francis Bernard of Massachusetts, no less, was one; he wanted Mount Desert Island as payment in lieu of cash for out-of-pocket expenses owed him by the colony. To secure his claim he needed to fulfill three requirements: royal confirmation of his grant, people to settle on his land, and a survey of the island. Bernard was gratified when Abraham Somes and James Richardson accepted his offer of free land and settled their families at what is now Somesville, the first permanent settlement on Mount Desert Island. Ebenezer Sutton fared well, too, having obtained the island that now bears his name in exchange for two quarts of rum! Other, uninvited, settlers came, and benefited from the governor's largess when he surveyed land, built houses, and gave lots to each of the families there. Royal approval of Sir Francis' grant was finally obtained in 1771.

But all of Bernard's plans came to nothing when the onset of the American Revolution made his loyalty to the king a black mark against him and provoked Americans to confiscate his land title. Bernard prudently returned to England and his reward by the king of the title of baronet.

When the war was over and American independence established, two claimants to Mount Desert Island appeared: One was Sir John Bernard, the governor's son, who claimed his father's property on the basis that the land was willed to him before the American government had confiscated it. The General Court of Massachusetts (to which Maine belonged until 1820), influenced by the fact that Bernard Jr. had joined the American cause during the conflict and had remained loyal to it, granted him the western half of the island in 1785.

The second claimant was Marie Therese de Gregoire, aristocratic granddaughter of Sieur de la Mothe Cadillac. Falling on hard times because of the unrest in France following the success of the American Revolution, Madame de Gregoire petitioned the Court for possession of the island, a claim she based on her grandfather's land claim of 1688. Although Cadillac's grant had been rescinded at the Treaty of Utrecht in 1713, the court—impelled by kindly sentiment toward France and influenced by letters from that friend of the revolution, Lafayette—eventually accorded her the eastern half of the island.

RUSSELL D. BUTCHER

The greater yellowlegs and other migrating shore birds often congregate in the mudflats and marshes at Thompson Island.

The ocean's booming voice resounds at Thunder Hole, a chasm carved by tide and surf.

RON GUSTAFSON

Thus it was that Mount Desert Island, split by the authority of the pen, became the property of the son of a colonial English governor and the granddaughter of a French adventurer. Bernard, apparently lacking in proper gratitude, promptly mortgaged his half of the island and returned to England, where he pledged his loyalty to the king and forgot Mount Desert for all time.

But Madame de Grégoire and her husband settled down at Hulls Cove on Mount Desert, where they built a house and mill. Failing at farming, they eked out a precarious existence by selling off parcels of their land. By 1806 the de Grégoires had become so poor that they had to sell off their house and all remaining property. A few years later wife and husband were buried at Hulls Cove, where "under a bit of rough granite . . . they lie possessed in death of an infinitesimal portion of their once extensive domain. . . ."

Bernard and the de Grégoires had rapidly sold their landholdings to non-resident landlords. But their real-estate interests and financial affairs probably made very little difference to the ever-increasing number of settlers who homesteaded Mount Desert and adjacent islands. Those who could afford it bought titles to their land; others just squatted, probably feeling secure in the knowledge that their absentee owners would not bother to evict them.

THE SETTLERS

By 1820, in this remote place of islands and sea, farming and lumbering vied with fishing and shipbuilding as the major occupations. Settlers converted hundreds of acres of trees into wood products ranging from schooners and barns to baby cribs and hand tools. Farmers in the timeless cycle of the seasons seeded the land and harvested wheat, rye, corn, and potatoes. By 1850 the familiar sights of fishermen and deep-water sailors, fish racks and shipyards revealed a way of life and breed of people intimately linked to the sea. Ships from Mount Desert and nearby islands sailed the fishing banks, the coastal routes, and even the distant oceans.

Crews of storm-tossed ships were often lost at sea, and wives and daughters were comforted by neighbors who knew too well that their own hardy husbands, brothers, and sons would be as frail as matchsticks in any contest with a sea gone mad.

Despite these recurring disasters, life went on. Schools, churches, and roads were built, and town governments that would eventually become models of democracy were established. Steadfast, industrious, and above all self-reliant, the people of Mount Desert knew the country would give to them only what they themselves had put into it—with their wits, determination, and sweat.

ED ELVIDGE

ANIMALS ANIMALS/JOHN STEEL

A lobster trap (usually a slatted oak case fitted with netting) is divided into two partitions, "kitchen" and "parlor." Attracted by a bait bag filled with dead fish, the lobster (a scavenger) enters the kitchen through a funnel-shaped entrance—the "eye"—which prevents it from backing out. In its attempt to leave, the lobster crawls through another eye into the parlor, which has no exit. A bright buoy, secured to the trap by a line, bobs on the water's surface. Its distinctive markings identify it as the property of one of Maine's many lobstermen, who must register their "colors" with the state. Traps are checked at least once every other day and may contain several lobsters. Our esteem for lobsters was not shared by all our forebears. In early New England, a bond servant felt himself lucky if he didn't have to eat lobster more than twice weekly!

ED ELVIDGE

ED ELVIDGE

In the popular mind the word "pioneer" may evoke an image of a family traveling westward in a canvas-topped wagon. But this is only half the picture. The roots of America's pioneer heritage were nourished not only on the plains, mountains, and deserts of the West, but also right here, on the Maine coast, as far east as one can get on the United States mainland.

William and Hannah Gilley were classic examples of this kind of spirit. In 1806 they camped on spruce-clad Baker Island four miles by sea from Mount Desert, built a house and barn and

Built in 1858, Bass Harbor Head Light marks the entrance to Blue Hill Bay. For those who "go down to the sea," lighthouses symbolize security, sympathy, and never-ceasing watchfulness.

ED ELVIDGE

grew nearly everything they needed to eat and wear, including forage for their fifty sheep and a few cattle, hogs, and chickens. They caught herring and mackerel and picked up lobsters in the shallows. Their skilled hands wielded the axe, guided the plow, trimmed the sails, threaded the spinning wheel.

The Gilleys had twelve children, all of whom lived to maturity. Mrs. Gilley knew the values to be found in books and taught her offspring to read, write, and cipher. On fine summer Sundays, she and the children attended church at Southwest Harbor, no small task considering that they had to row seven miles from and to their island home.

In 1828 the federal government constructed a lighthouse on Baker Island. William became its first keeper, a post he held for twenty-one years.

THE RUSTICATORS

The Gilleys and many other practical, hardworking islanders of their breed brought function and utility to its highest form. But it was the outsiders—the artists and journalists—who proclaimed the beauties of this country to the world. In 1844 Thomas Cole, a partisan of the Hudson

River school of painting, glorified Mount Desert with brush and pen, inspiring his patrons and friends in New York, who began to flock here to see for themselves the island that had inspired such beautiful canvasses.

By 1850 Mount Desert had become an artist's mecca. So enamored of the island was Frederic Church, like Cole a landscape artist, that he returned to spend at least seven summers in attempting to capture on canvas the elusive roar and motion of sea and surf. Magazines featured his work, and word of Mount Desert's wild beauty reached an ever-expanding circle of nature lovers, campers, students, and sportsmen who came to experience it for themselves.

These were the "rusticators." Undaunted by the crude accommodations and simple food, all that was available, they sought out local fishermen and farmers to put them up in exchange for a modest fee. The typical Acadian, always in need of a little extra cash, was quick to don the role of part-time innkeeper, sharing his rooms, the abundant lobster, and the wife's homemade donuts. Summer after summer the rusticators returned to renew friendships with the plain folk of the island and, most of all, to savor again and

In 1887, Bar Harbor supported 17 hotels, but by 1890 the cottage era was in full swing and twenty years later the old hotel days were gone for good. The wealthy cottagers demanded—and got—the pleasures of tennis, golf, swimming, and yacht racing. "They also founded clubs such as the Bar Harbor Reading Room where under the Maine prohibition law most of the 'reading' was done through the bottom of a glass."

Kennarden Lodge was built in 1892 by John S. Kennedy, banker and railroad man. No "cottage" was exactly like another—each projected the taste of its owner—but collectively they typified an era of elegance and ostentation. Extravagance probably reached its climax in 1925 when E. T. Stotesbury built his 80-room mansion containing 28 bathrooms, 26 marble fireplaces, and 52 telephone lines.

BAR HARBOR HISTORICAL SOCIETY PHOTO. CIRCA 1900

again "the bounteous feast which nature spread before them." And in addition to the scenery and the picnicking, there were the more pulse-quickening joys of boating, buckboarding, and mountain-climbing activities.

Such high spirits enticed increasing numbers of kindred souls to share this summer Shangri-la, and eventually the surge of newcomers increased to the point that the capacity of the islanders to house and feed them became severely taxed. After about 1860, free enterprise stepped in to take up the slack. Hotels were built, easing the demand for rooms at the traditional "farmhouse," and by 1880 thirty hotels—most simple and rather bare but always full—competed for the vacationer's dollar. Steamboats, some of whose names became familiar household words, plied regular runs up and down the Maine coast to facilitate the steady flow of visitors to its harbors.

Tourism was rapidly taking its place as a major industry while other island industries, notably lumbering, declined. After the excellent quality of the granite of the western shore of Somes Sound was discovered, this granite became highly prized for use in many of the important buildings in New England and Washington, giving rise to a quarry operation that thrived in the late nineteenth century and thereafter maintained a limited activity until the last decade or so.

The Summer People

For a select handful of Americans, the 1880s and the "Gay Nineties" meant affluence enjoyed on a scale without precedent. Mount Desert, then still remote from the fast-growing cities of the East, was a favorite retreat for the socially and politically prominent people of the times. Wealthy citizens such as the Rockefellers, Morgans, Fords, Vanderbilts, Carnegies, and Astors—to mention only a few of the most famous—chose to spend their summers here, forgetting for a few months the increasing tempo of big business and accompanying pressures back in the hot cities.

Not content with the simple lodgings then available, these families transformed the landscape of Mount Desert Island with their elegant estates, establishments that boasted stately mansions (euphemistically called "cottages"), formal gardens, and clipped, spacious lawns. Eventually more than two hundred of these cottages graced the island's shoreline between Bar Harbor and Somes Sound, changing the flavor of the islands from one of rusticity to that of a genteel society.

Major eastern stores followed their rich clienteles by establishing shops that catered to expensive tastes. Luxury, refinement, and ostentatious behavior replaced the "earlier rudeness of board and lodging" and the informality of early days. The season was filled with dinner dances, musicales, yachting parties—all replacing the buckboard rides and picnics of an earlier era. The summer boarder, no longer free to roam the island at will, either bought a place for himself or wandered on to some other resort.

Life for the cottager was a constant social whirl (often so hectic that, ironically, many families built "camps" on other parts of the island in order to occasionally get away from it all). Plush carriages harnessed to handsome horses carried richly dressed men and women to tennis matches, gala balls, or other social events of the day. After-noon teas were especially popular, and teahouses sprang up as meeting places for the gregarious society of Mount Desert. (That tradition continued until June 21, 1979, when fire destroyed Jordan Pond House, then the only remaining teahouse on the island. Reconstructed in 1982, the new Jordan Pond House carries on the tradition of the old, so that again—in the sedate atmosphere of the past—diners can partake of the superb chicken and lobster, fresh popovers, and homemade ice cream for which the teahouse was famous.)

For over forty years, the wealthy held sway at Mount Desert, escalating it into an internationally known resort. "Millionaire's Row," as the ocean frontage between Bar Harbor and Salisbury Cove became known, boosted the local economy with its lavish entertaining. "Mrs. Edward Stotesbury gave parties on a scale that required the ordering of champagne glasses through a local emporium in lots of fifty dozen." But the Great Depression and the ensuing discipline of World War II staged the beginning of the end for such extravagance. Many of the grand houses became burdens to maintain, and some owners turned them over to charitable organizations. The Atwater Kent mansion *Sonogee*, for example, became a Bar Harbor nursing home.

The final disastrous blow came in 1947, when a fire of monumental proportions, whipped to a furor by eighty-mile winds from the northwest, swept the countryside in great sheets. Before such a satanic force, nothing could stand. Forests were leveled, mountains seared, and many of the great estates of the wealthy consumed in a matter of minutes. It took five days to bring the fire under control, five days that brought an era to an end finally and forever.

But left alone, nature heals, and eventually the scarred and dismal landscape seemed almost "as if new-created in all the freshness of childhood." Some of the great mansions remain. Today they are stately witnesses to a time when Mount Desert was a gracious and generous host to the wealthy at leisure.

SUGGESTED READING

Eliot, Charles W. *John Gilley of Baker's Island*. Philadelphia: Eastern National Park and Monument Ass'n., 1978. Originally published in *The Century Magazine*, 1899. (Available only at park)

Morison, Samuel E. *The Story of Mount Desert Island*. Boston: Little, Brown and Co., 1960.

Acadia Today

Acadia is a land that inspires poetry in the most prosaic of souls. Here is room, glorious room to revel in the opulence of nature at her freest and best, whatever mood may set the scene from day to day.

Blue skies dip low to define islands, peninsulas, and a sea that stretches to a far horizon. Sailing yachts share the rise and fall of the waves with fishing boats. Clusters of gaily painted buoys dip and nod, marking the places where slatted, baited wooden traps rest on the sea floor, awaiting the tasty lobster, the star attraction of Maine dinners. On the surface, harbor porpoises —one of several kinds of whales found in Acadian waters—crest the waves in a graceful ballet.

A harbor seal bobs in the swells; its short muzzle and glowing, gentle eyes are puppylike in their appeal.

Birds are everywhere. Guillemots (known colloquially as "sea pigeons"), small and dark with white wing patches, scatter as the boats advance. The long-necked cormorant, sometimes mistaken for a large duck, perches on ledges with outstretched wings or floats low in the water like a soaked sponge. The osprey, that king of fishermen, is awesome in its dive: folding its wings it plummets head-first into the water, emerging a few seconds later with its prey in its talons. And then there is that most exciting of all birds, the bald eagle, rising silently from its aerie or drifting regally on an upward current of air in Frenchman Bay.

Lighthouses, such as the one at Baker Island, affirm that Acadia is not always postcard bright. For when the warm south wind blows across the chilly Atlantic, rafts of fog dissolve earth and sky into a ghostly gray, a misty scene that is fully as satisfying to the true romantic as the brilliant hues of Acadia's sun-drenched days. This is when the lighthouse becomes more than just "picturesque"; indeed its warning beacon is the most real thing in sight and the sonorous bellow of its foghorn is a comforting companion in the gloom.

The evergreen forests of Acadia create a different mood, but one that complements sea and rocky coast. The rustle of leaves and the wind in the branches have not changed in a million years, and the words "forest primeval" leap easily to mind. Since humans entered the scene, kinship with the forest has been a special and a constant

RUSSELL D. BUTCHER

This picturesque wood-frame post office on the wharf at Great Cranberry Island is an important part of island life.

The nimble fingers of these young blueberry lovers reap the generous harvest of nature within view of massive Duck Brook Bridge.

thing. Just a whiff of the pungent odor of balsam or the clean smell of spruce will evoke images of a pristine beauty that is immediately spirit-lifting.

The silence, almost palpable here, is broken only by the occasional chattering of a red squirrel or the hiss-like "tsee, tsee, tsee" of a golden-crowned kinglet. The forest is bathed in a light that is ethereal; even at midday, tree branches shield out the sun—except here and there where a space created by a storm-uprooted giant allows columns of light to burst through, illumining a carpet of needles and searching out bunchberry, starflower, and lily-of-the-valley. At Otter Point, *Usnea* (a mosslike lichen more commonly known as "prophet's beard") entangles the twigs and branches of the evergreens. Hanging in long, wispy strands, the lichens, washed frequently in rain and fog, add a touch of hoary age.

Acadia's evergreen forests consist chiefly of balsam fir and red spruce, but along the immediate coast stretches a thin belt of white spruce. Emigrants from farther north, they appear to prosper in the cold, wet drafts spawned out over the icy North Atlantic.

Yet even in the seemingly ageless spruce-fir forests, there is change—change that can happen as quickly as the toppling of a tree by a powerful gale or as slowly as the splitting of bedrock by probing roots. The great fire of 1947 was the most rapid of the changes to affect the forests in historic times, transforming roughly the eastern third of Mount Desert Island into smoke and ashes. Starting October 17 near Hulls Cove, after a summer of drought, the inferno enveloped over 17,000 acres before the waters of the coast at Great Head extinguished its raging fury.

Today stumps and snags bearing charcoal scars are evidences of the destructive energy unleashed by that fire. But in the ensuing years a new deciduous forest sprang from the scorched earth; spruce and fir yielded to grey birch, trembling aspen, big-toothed aspen, and other sun-loving trees formerly shaded out by the big trees. After the fire, myriad delicate, windborne seeds

White-tailed deer are common in Acadia, and wary. Born in late spring, a week-old fawn can easily outrun a man. It will retain its spots for about three months.

A sharp "chuck-chuck-chuck" identifies the voice of the eastern chipmunk.

A red fox sniffs for his supper. His reddish coat is common, but other color phases do occur.

The black body and narrow white stripe up the center forehead unmistakably brand this appealing trio as striped skunks.

Red spruces tower beyond a luxurious bouquet of cinnamon ferns. Both species of plants are widely distributed throughout Acadia.

spread over the wounded land, sprouted, and daubed the barren landscape with a riot of vivacious colors.

Aspen and birch are short-lived, however, and the shadows of the parent trees deny life-giving light to their own seedlings. So the spruce, which grows readily under the canopy of these "nurse" trees, is even now reclaiming territory lost in the fire. Given time, the murmur of spruces may drown out the whisper of aspens and birches.

Historically speaking, deer have always lived on Mount Desert Island, but their numbers increased following the great fire because, by and large, they preferred to browse the deciduous plants that sprang up on the burned-over land. The flash of the white-tailed deer's upright "flag," a hoof imprint in the soft earth, or the fresh break where a twig has been nipped from a red-maple seedling or blueberry bush may be the only evidence of its fleeting presence.

Another favorite, the vegetarian beaver, of-

GLENN VAN NIMWEGEN

This durable lodge and stout dam of mud and sticks illustrate the considerable engineering skills of the beaver. The thick fur, webbed hind feet, and flat tail provide the beaver with warmth, speed, and mobility. Like all rodents, its teeth never stop growing, obliging it to a lifetime of gnawing.

A seldom-seen resident, the river otter

ANIMALS ANIMALS/STOUFFER PRODUCTIONS, LTD.

An amiable bandit, the raccoon

RON GUSTAFSON

TED GRINDLE

ANIMALS ANIMALS/WM. D. GRIFFIN

The white-throated sparrow is a beloved resident of Acadia. A bird-watcher's paradise, Mount Desert boasts over 300 species. The island's diverse habitats—forests, ocean, mud flats, marshes, islands, bogs, meadows, and mountains—accommodate about 140 species of breeding birds, including 21 species of warblers.

ten appeases his appetite by munching the inner bark and tender twigs of the aspen. These large, amphibious, flat-tailed rodents have strung their dams across virtually every brook in the deciduous forest. The ponds formed behind their dams may evict some of the beaver's wildlife neighbors —ground-nesting birds, mice, and other creatures—by flooding their homes. But the ponds also provide a place where trout find a cool haven on hot summer days, green herons stalk minnows, frogs serenade, and mosquitoes hatch.

At Acadia, trails that may begin in the forest often lead to the edge of the sea. The tang of the salt air begins to mask the fragrance of balsam as wooded paths near the shore. A window of light streams through the forest wall; beyond the trees lie the rock shore and the ocean itself. The lines of Longfellow memorized as a child take on meaning now as "loud from its rocky caverns, the deep-voiced neighboring ocean speaks, and in accents disconsolate answers the wail of the forest."

TIDES EBB AND FLOW

Tides, continually moving up and down the shore at intervals of 6 hours and 12 minutes, have made water the dominating physical force at the ocean's edge. For rather complex reasons involving topography of the ocean floor, currents, and irregularities in the coast, tides vary in height. At Acadia they average 11 to 12 feet. But twice each month, when the sun and moon pull in line, the tides may reach 14 feet in height, hence the expression *spring tides*, describing a time when the sea springs high upon the earth. When the moon and sun are at right angles to one another, however, their opposing gravitational forces produce tides only 8 or 9 feet high. These are *neap* (a Norse word meaning "barely touching") *tides*.

At ebb tide, water withdrawn from the land exposes horizontal bands of barnacles seemingly as inert as the rocks on which they cluster. Below them wet mats of limp, unkempt seaweed or of algae—green, brown, and red—festoon craggy

Harbor seals often bask on offshore ledges and islands. On land they seem ungainly because their rear flippers cannot be turned forward to walk. But in the water the seals are transformed into graceful, agile creatures; aided by the bullet shape of their torsos, well padded with insulating blubber.

Acorn barnacles—related to crabs and lobsters, all crustaceans—encrust the rocky shore in fairly definite zones. At flood tide, a hand-like feeding appendage reaches through the open, limy plates to filter plankton.

rock faces. Crabs, periwinkles, and dog whelks hide among these plants, seeking refuge from dryness and marauding gulls.

In the tide pools (pockets of sea water left in rock basins), sea urchins resembling green pincushions graze motionlessly on the pastures of algae; even a starfish with tentacles embracing a mussel in a grip of death is a study in stillness. Although the tide pool protects its inhabitants from exposure to air, its microenvironment may be severely tested by sun and rain. As the water evaporates, salinity increases, and as the temperature rises, oxygen decreases. On the other hand, showers may dilute the salt levels to intolerable levels.

Even the incoming tide is a threat to some creatures, who must hang on or get washed out to

TED GRINDLE

The bold, gregarious herring gull is about as common in Acadia as sea water! It is a full-time scavenger but also feeds on crabs, mollusks, and sea urchins.

sea. To avoid such a disaster, the barnacle secretes a glue-like substance that binds itself to the rock. Although a hammer blow can easily smash the barnacle's limestone shell, the conical shape of the shell serves to disperse the energy of waves. The blue mussel, often so congested that it is difficult to insert a fingernail between individuals, anchors itself by means of touch filaments, or *byssal* threads. Starfish and sea urchins grasp support with their numerous tube feet; periwinkles, dog whelks, and limpets clamp down, sealing themselves to the rocky substrate.

Despite the perils of pounding waves, the rising tide returns to renew life on the rocky shore. Seaweeds, no longer prostrate, bend and reach as the surf strokes their feathery fronds. Recharged with water, the barnacle opens its shell and extends a plumed appendage. Like an agile baseball catcher, it uses its lacy mitt to snatch plankton from the sea and waft it into its mouth. The onrushing waters distribute oxygen, remove wastes, scatter eggs and spores, and level climatic extremes between summer and winter. As Rachel Carson has written: "When we go down to the low-tide line, we enter a world that is as old as the earth itself—the primeval meeting place of the elements of earth and water, a place of compromise and conflict and eternal change."

Acadia—soft as fog, hard as granite, bold as a gull, gentle as a fawn—is a land that lures the traveler with charms as diverse as those offered by any of our national parks. But people who come here through a love of the sea are not immune to the appeal of the forests; and people who think only of climbing Cadillac Mountain find themselves wondering about the strange marine world far below. Therein lies the charm and magnetism of Acadia National Park, a place of beauty and repose that is intact largely through the wisdom and foresight of one man—but that is yet another story in the colorful history of Acadia.

GLENN VAN NIMWEGEN

Dog whelks are carnivorous snails.

George B. Dorr, "father of Acadia National Park," (left) converses with Charles W. Eliot, president of Harvard University, in this early 1900's photo taken on the shore of Jordan Pond. In 1901 Eliot, Dorr, and other prominent citizens established the "Hancock County Trustees of Public Reservations," an organization whose purpose was to preserve points of interest on Mount Desert for public use. Land bought by the trustees later became a gift to the nation with the establishment of Acadia National Park.

NPS PHOTO

A tree-lined trail skirts to the right of the aptly named lake, the "Bowl," before ascending the "Beehive," a mountain whose name suggests the shape of its glacially carved east face.

The Making of a Park

Although the affluent of the turn of the century came here primarily to frolic, they had much to do with preserving the landscape that we know today. The presence of their great estates checked the progress of industries (notably lumbering)—progress that, it might be reasonably speculated, may otherwise have harmed the Acadian landscape irreversibly.

But the influence of the elitists was more than just accidental. These were people who had been raised on the philosophies of Emerson and Thoreau and the romantic sagas of poets such as Maine's own Henry Wadsworth Longfellow. Thus imbued with a love of nature and its beauties, they were disposed from birth to revere and preserve the natural character of the island.

It was from this social strata that a tireless spokesman for the cause of conservation came. His name was George B. Dorr, a tall, lean man with a walrus mustache, who often appeared stylishly if casually dressed in baggy tweeds. Scion of an old Boston family and a bachelor, he read Homer for relaxation—in the original Greek! For 43 years Dorr devoted his life, energy, and family fortune (textiles) to furthering the cause of preserving the Acadian countryside. Four million visitors a year now enjoy the fruits of Dorr's tireless labors in their behalf.

Dorr's lifelong quest began in 1901, at a meeting with Charles W. Eliot (president of Harvard University) and ten other concerned citizens. Disturbed by the growing development of the Bar Harbor area, the group formed the "Hancock County Trustees of Public Reservations." The corporation, whose sole purpose was to preserve points of interest for the perpetual use of the public, elected Eliot its president and Dorr its executive officer and purchasing agent.

The year 1908 saw the first significant donations: "The Beehive," a 520-foot, ice-scalloped hill overlooking Sand Beach, and to the north of the Beehive a little mountain lake lying in a basin scooped out of the granite and appropriately called "The Bowl." Both parcels were donated by Mrs. Charles Homan of Boston.

Encouraged by this good fortune and galvanized into action by the dangers he foresaw in the newly invented gasoline-powered portable sawmill, the dynamic Dorr resolved to obtain Cadillac Mountain. This acquisition, accomplished with the financial aid of his fellow trustee John S. Kennedy, was to become the centerpiece of the national park that would one day attract visitors from all over the world.

But acquiring land wasn't an easy task. Occasionally Dorr's efforts would result in a "photo-finish" victory, accomplished only a few minutes before a land option was due to expire. Whether he was successful or not in some endeavor might thus depend upon the speed of his carriage as much as upon his persuasive manner. But whatever the circumstances of these endeavors, it was Dorr's energy and drive that brought in gift after gift and enlarged the holdings of the infant cor-

A portion of the 57-mile carriage road system—legacy to the park of John D. Rockefeller, Jr.—rambles serenely along the east shore of Little Long Pond.

poration until in 1912 its trustees had acquired over 5,000 acres, including a parcel donated by Dorr himself.

Over the years Dorr proved to be as adept at parrying threats to his beloved enterprise as he was at expanding its boundaries. In midwinter, 1913, for example, ominous news hurriedly dispatched him to Augusta: the Maine legislature had introduced a bill to repeal the corporation's tax-free status. In typical fashion, Dorr marshaled enough political muscle to kill the bill, but when he entrained back to Boston, he was beset by uncertainty. What if the charter was again challenged? The thing to do, he concluded, was to let the government itself protect the preserve. "It is here," Dorr later wrote, "the story of our national park begins, born of the attack upon our Public Reservations charter."

For Dorr to attain his goal meant immersion into politics and a lot of plain hard work. At first it meant even giving up the idea of offering the land to the government under the label "national park." In the spring of 1914 many constituents

Cobblestone Bridge, spanning Jordan Stream, was built in 1917, the first in a series of 16 bridges linking the carriage roads. The rustic, massive 140-foot span is richly textured with cobblestones set in a masonry foundation. The single round arch is flanked by great buttresses that serve as observation platforms.

GLENN VAN NIMWEGEN

Deer Brook Bridge curves gracefully over its namesake. Set into the spandrel between its twin arches is a plain circular medallion bearing the date of the bridge's construction, 1925.

GLENN VAN NIMWEGEN

were beseiging Congress with proposals to establish national parks. Dorr was a seasoned fighter in the political arena, and he feared these proposals would be lumped together in one bill and the whole lot defeated. So he instead decided to offer the now 6,000 acres as a national *monument*, which could be created by the president, acting alone, without endorsement by Congress.

The Public Land Commission, however, would not approve the corporation's donation until the land titles and deeds held by the trustees were verified. It took two laborious years to sift through the various abstracts involved, but when he returned to Washington in the spring of 1916, the commission found everything in order. After more delays, caused by the question of the legality of the government's acceptance of a gift from a private corporation, the way was finally clear for the President, on July 16, 1916, to announce the creation of *Sieur de Monts National Monument*.

Still not satisfied, Dorr at 63, rather than retiring, tenaciously renewed his labors to obtain full national park status for his beloved preserve. Once again he summoned support from his powerful political friends, including Theodore Roosevelt, who dashed off a timely letter aimed at clearing a bottleneck in the house appropriations committee.

As part of the carriage-road network, on what was then his private estate, Rockefeller constructed huge gates at the two places where the carriage roads intersected public motor routes—at Jordan Pond and at Brown Mountain (depicted here). Attached to each pair of gates, the "gatekeeper's house" permitted Rockefeller and his neighbors easy access to the public roads.

Soon after Maine's congressional delegation introduced the bill, Congress approved it, and on February 26, 1919, President Woodrow Wilson signed the act establishing the nation's first national park east of the Mississippi. Dorr fittingly became its first superintendent. Comprised entirely of private gifts, the park bore the name *Lafayette,* acknowledging the country's strong Francophile feelings during World War I.

Ten years after Lafayette came into existence, the park boundaries were extended to reach across Frenchman Bay to embrace Schoodic Peninsula. But this was not accomplished without complications. The donors of the land were of strong pro-British sentiment and demurred at granting land to a preserve bearing a French name. To Dorr a park known by any other name was still a park—and an even larger one if it were to include Schoodic. Besides, he said, he actually preferred the suggested name *Acadia,* even though to change the park's name and allow for donations outside Mount Desert Island would require an act of Congress. But the irrepressible veteran of political stratagems knew well how to gain allegiance in the public arena. Congress consented to the change, and on January 19, 1929, President Calvin Coolidge rescinded the park name and proclaimed it *Acadia National Park.*

A wealthy man's dream had become the common man's playground. Dorr's labors constituted "the greatest of one-man shows in the history of land conservation." When he died in 1944 he left not only a legacy of land but also "a memory of courage and perseverance, of patience (another word for good manners), and of a respect for inviolate beauty and a willingness to fight for its continuity."

ROCKEFELLER AND THE CARRIAGE ROADS

Acadia demonstrates, probably more than any other park, the creative partnership between private citizens and government. It is a legacy from conservationists willing to expend a great deal of time, energy, and money in order to preserve the quiet pleasures of a consoling landscape for their own and future generations. No person better exemplifies this philanthropic ideal at Acadia than John D. Rockefeller, Jr. Rejecting the notion that his great wealth was for the benefit of his family only, he gave donations—starting with $100 in 1911 and resulting at the time of his death in a total of 10,700 acres—that account for almost one-third of Acadia's acreage today. Among his investments in public trust is the magnificent stretch from Sand Beach to Otter Point, now tra-

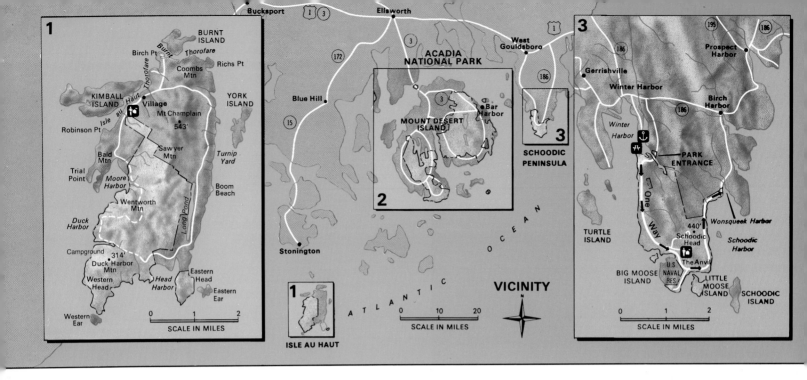

versed by Ocean Drive, a road that he had rebuilt during the 1930s.

Rockefeller had a mania for building roads. In 1913, he conceived the idea of constructing carriage roads in order to make accessible to the public the lovely vistas that would become Acadia National Park. The 57 miles of roads (51 miles in the park and 6 on adjacent lands) that comprise the park system testify to his artistry, sense of location, and esthetic awareness. Even the stone culverts, ditches, and retaining walls that define the edges of the roadways proclaim Rockefeller's creative instincts.

The roads wander aimlessly and delightfully. One breaches the talus slope on the west bank of Jordan Pond; another climbs high on the shoulder of Sargent Mountain, then drops down to hug the shore of Upper Hadlock Pond; still another en-

circles Eagle Lake. Wherever the roads may lead, they gently beguile one with a sense of solitude and an appreciation of the harmony present in nature.

Sixteen stone bridges ornament the carriage-road system. Carefully cut by masons into graceful, flowing curves, each bridge announces itself with its own special combination of balustrades, turrets, arches, and piers. The first bridge, built in 1917, spans Jordan Stream; the last, built in 1933, stands astride the Stanley Brook entrance to Acadia.

Rockefeller planned the carriage roads as an alternative to the main road system and competition with motor vehicles. Today, in the spirit of that tradition, park users can peacefully hike, bicycle, and ride horseback—free from the uproar of the "infernal" combustion engine.

Duck Brook Bridge is a three-arch tour de force completed in 1929. Like its sister bridges, it was constructed of hand-hewn granite in a long, laborious process. Reflecting on his building achievements, Rockefeller allegedly remarked that the bridges might as well have been built of diamonds for all they cost him. Today most park visitors would agree that the results—Acadia's handsome bridges—were well worth the effort and the cost.

ACADIA NATIONAL PARK

TO ELLSWORTH
Bar Harbor Airport
THOMPSON ISLAND
Information Center
THOMAS ISLAND
Thomas Harbor
NARROWS
Hadley Point
THOMAS ISLAND
Hamilton Pond
EASTERN BAY
Sand Point
Salisbury Cove
Parker Point
FRENCHMAN
Lookout Pt
Hulls Cove
Hulls Cove
VISITOR CENTER
BURNT PORCUPINE
LONG PORCUPINE ISLAND

Jones Marsh
ALLEY ISLAND
Town Hill
Fawn Pond
YARMOUTH N.S. FERRY
BAR ISLAND
SHEEP PORCUPINE
Passable at Low Tide

WESTERN BAY
Indian Point
GREEN ISLAND
Youngs Mountain 680'
Witch Hole Pond
Breakneck Ponds
BAR HARBOR
BALD PORCUPINE

BLACK ISLAND
M O U N T   D E S E R T
Park Headquarters
BAY

Deep Cove
SQUID ISLAND
Somesville
Somes Pond
Aunt Betty Pond
Eagle Lake
Sieur de Monts Spring
Nature Center
Jackson Laboratory
THE THRUMCAP

TLETT AND
Round Pond
BAR ISLAND
Dorr Mountain 1270'
One Way
OCEAN DRIVE (One Way)

Pretty Marsh
I S L A N D
SOMES SOUND
Sargent Mountain 1373'
The Bubbles
Cadillac 1530' Mountain
1058' Champlain Mtn.
Schooner Head

Pretty Marsh Harbor
Long Pond
Hall Quarry
Bubble Pond
The Bowl

FOLLY SLAND
Hodgdon Pond
Echo Lake
681' Acadia Mountain
852' Norumbega Mountain
1248' Pemetic Mountain
520' The Beehive
Great Head

Beech Mountain 839'
St. Sauveur Mountain 679'
Valley Cove
1194' Penobscot Mtn
Upper Hadlock Pond
Jordan Pond House
.698' The Triad
Gorham Mountain
Sand Beach
Thunder Hole
Otter Cliffs

Seal Cove Pond
Western Mountain 1071'
Fernald Point
Lower Hadlock Pond
Long Pond
Day Mountain
Otter Creek
Black Woods
Otter Point
Otter Cove

Seal Cove
Seal Cove
SEE
Northeast Harbor
Northeast Harbor
Seal Harbor
Seal Harbor
Western Point
Hunters Head
Ingraham Pt.

BLUE HILL BAY
West Tremont
Southwest Harbor
BEAR ISLAND
GREENING ISLAND
SUTTON IS

Bernard
Manset
Bass Harbor
Big Heath
Seawall
Ship Harbor
SWAN ISLAND FERRY
Bass Harbor Head

ISLESFORD HISTORICAL MUSEUM
Islesford
LITTLE CRANBERRY ISLAND
GREAT CRANBERRY ISLAND
BAKER ISLAND

O C E A N
A T L A N T I C

SCALE IN MILES
0   1   2

NOTE: Private property rights MUST be respected

Swimming
Lighthouse
Ranger Station
Ferry

Campground
Picnic Area
Fire Lookout
Interpretive Trail

Auto Tour Road
Paved Road
Unpaved Road
Carriage Path
Park Area (Approx)

The Heritage of Acadia

Mariners and missionaries, pioneers and rusticators, cottagers and conservationists—all played important roles in the romantic past of Acadia. Their stories are the threads that weave the stirring events and the poignant moments of yesteryear into the fabric of Acadian history.

Within its boundaries can be traced the initial assault on a wilderness, the early struggles of farmers and fishermen to wrest a living from land and sea, the idyllic memories of an age whose innocence and opulence can never be recaptured.

The simple pleasures of "ocean and land, woodland, lake, and mountains" that over the centuries have been sought and found by millions from all over the world are still here. Once only a landmark on Champlain's rude map, Acadia has become a landmark in the chronicles of conservation. Because of this, her glorious vistas will continue into the future, to be enjoyed by millions more to come—in the constant pursuit of that precious and elusive thing we call *contentment*.

SUGGESTED READING

BUTCHER, RUSSELL D. *Field Guide to Acadia National Park, Maine.* New York: Reader's Digest Press, 1977.

BUTCHER, RUSSELL D., AND MENZIETTI, MARIE IVEY. *Maine Paradise.* New York: Penguin Books, 1976.

CARSON, RACHEL. *The Edge of the Sea.* Boston: Houghton Mifflin Co., 1955.

COMAN, DALE REX. *The Native Mammals, Reptiles and Amphibians of Mount Desert Island, Maine.* Philadelphia: Univ. of Pennsylvania, 1972.

TILDEN, FREEMAN. *The National Parks.* New York: Alfred A. Knopf, Inc., 1976.

ED ELVIDGE

Yachts rest at anchor in a fog-bound harbor.

This monolith of Schoodic Peninsula granite was sculpted by the furious hand of the surging sea. Photo by Ed Cooper.

Back cover: The splendor of Sand Beach stretches invitingly between forest-draped highlands. Photo by David Muench.

Created, Designed, and Published in the U.S.A.
Printed by Tien Wah Press (Pte.) Ltd, Singapore